AF824183

What I Want You to Have

Let Family Know®

This planner belongs to:

Let Family Know® LLC is dedicated to helping people organize the information that matters. The *What I want you to have Planner* is intended for planning purposes and making wishes known.

THIS PLANNER IS NOT LEGALLY BINDING, IS NOT A SUBSTITUTE FOR A WILL or changing a will – and should not be considered legal advice. Where legal matters are concerned, we urge you to seek advice from a professional attorney who is licensed to practice law in the state in which you reside.

ISBN 978-1-7334208-5-3

What I want you to have PLANNER

The *What I want you to have Planner* from Let Family Know® provides a place to note who you want to have your belongings if anything should happen to you.

This will help ensure your sentimental items will go to the rightful heirs. If there are items you cherish – maybe even family heirlooms – you may want to make time to complete some pages in this planner sooner than later. It will help make sure your family knows who you want to have them – and why. By briefly explaining why you're passing along a certain item to a specific person, you can help prevent hard feelings or strained relationships between siblings and family members at a difficult time when they need each other most.

Remember, this is not legally binding, but it can help protect your most important asset – your family.

Just a few tips

- **Use ink, and write legibly** so your instructions can be interpreted easily and accurately.
- **Where appropriate, write something about heritage items** that have been in the family for generations. Indicate if newer belongings are also ones you would like to keep in the family. Adding stories will help make them true legacy items.
- **Our words have the power to hurt or bless,** so write your entries carefully. Don't write in anger, or try to have the "last word" in old feuds. Instead, think about the legacy you leave. Be a blessing.

Did you know it's often things with less monetary value but a high emotional value that cause family rifts?

Let Family Know®

A few more tips

- **When listing items** provide as many details as needed to keep anyone from mistaking which item is in question – or who is to inherit it.
- **Do not go back and cross out** or write over the top of words, white words out, or erase anything written. Instead, use a fresh page to record changes to your plan as they occur.
- **Sign and date each entry upon completion.** You'll notice at the bottom of the back side of the page there's a simple witnessing feature. Although this feature does NOT make pages legally binding, having a witness can help validate your wishes should they ever be questioned.

Written by me	Date
Witnessed by me (optional)	Date

- **Be sure to fill in the person's name, item, date, and "page __ of __" on pages.** This will help keep entries intact if pages are removed and returned to the binder.
- **To prevent confusion,** pages are designed to use the same front and back for one item. For example, don't put grandma's earrings on the front and a motorcycle on the back.
- **If your description doesn't fill the page**, draw an X through the unfilled area. That will keep someone from adding information that would confuse or change your intention.
- **Completed pages can help an attorney or estate planner** to draw up formal, legally binding documents. Taking inventory of your belongings and organizing your thoughts before you meet will undoubtedly save a lot of time and legal fees.
- **To protect your wishes from accidental destruction,** copy pages from time to time and keep as a backup in a safe place outside of your home, like your bank safe deposit box. Or scan pages and store them digitally.

Want to add photos to your pages to support your wishes?

Some planner entries may be enhanced by attaching a photo, a copy of receipt or bill of sale, a copy of a letter, a copy of an appraisal, etc., to your Journal pages.

If so, there are many options for adhering them in a way that will ensure they stay attached. A visit to your local craft supply store, a search online, or talking with a person involved in scrapbooking or preserving memories and family histories, can provide you with suggestions for placing your photos on these pages. Be sure to keep your originals in a safe place, and attach only good quality copies.

You may also wish to reference digital media, a particular video, photo album, an online music or video collection, etc. If so, be sure to include the location of those items.

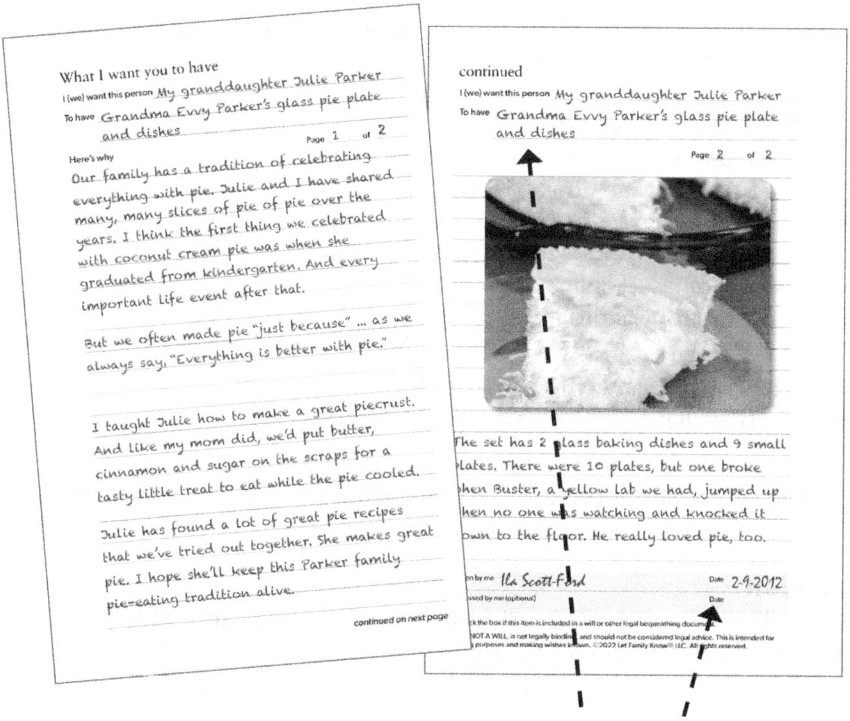
What I want you to have

I (we) want this person My granddaughter Julie Parker

To have Grandma Evvy Parker's glass pie plate and dishes

Page 1 of 2

Here's why

Our family has a tradition of celebrating everything with pie. Julie and I have shared many, many slices of pie of pie over the years. I think the first thing we celebrated with coconut cream pie was when she graduated from kindergarten. And every important life event after that.

But we often made pie "just because" ... as we always say, "Everything is better with pie."

I taught Julie how to make a great piecrust. And like my mom did, we'd put butter, cinnamon and sugar on the scraps for a tasty little treat to eat while the pie cooled.

Julie has found a lot of great pie recipes that we've tried out together. She makes great pie. I hope she'll keep this Parker family pie-eating tradition alive.

continued on next page

continued

I (we) want this person My granddaughter Julie Parker

To have Grandma Evvy Parker's glass pie plate and dishes

Page 2 of 2

The set has 2 glass baking dishes and 9 small lates. There were 10 plates, but one broke hen Buster, a yellow lab we had, jumped up hen no one was watching and knocked it own to the floor. He really loved pie, too.

n by me Ila Scott-Ford Date 2-9-2012

sed by me (optional) Date

k the box if this item is included in a will or other legal bequeathing docum

NOT A WILL, is not legally bindi and should not be considered legal advice. This is intended for purposes and making wishes known. ©2022 Let Family Know® LLC. All ghts reserved.

If you remove pages from the Journal and put them in a ring binder, be sure to continue the item's name, recipient, and page numbers so stories can be kept in tact when placing back in the binder. The pages numbers are for the individual item only, not for the entire Journal.

If you like the flexibility of adding, removing or rearranging pages, here's something you can do.

You can carefully take the pages out of this paperback book and put them into a ring binder. *If you're going to do this, it may be best to do it before writing begins.* An online search for "how to remove pages from a paperback book" will yield several results, including videos.

Heat gun/hair dryer approach
This will warm and loosen the glue holding the paperback book together.

1. Turn your hair dryer on using the higher heat setting. Carefully blow the hot air up and down along the book's spine. The dryer should not be touching the spine. It will take around 3 to 6 minutes to soften the glue so pages will remove easily.
2. When the glue is soft, gently pull the cover away from the spine. The entire cover should easily come off in one piece.
3. You may find it easier to remove the pages in sections. Try to keep them in order. It may be necessary to slightly reheat the glue on the spine of the pages so you can pull off any glue chunks, leaving a clean, smooth edge.
4. Once the pages and glue are removed, you're ready to punch the holes and place the pages in a ring binder. You can put the book covers in as well. Paper punches and planner-size ring binders can be purchased online or in an office supply store.

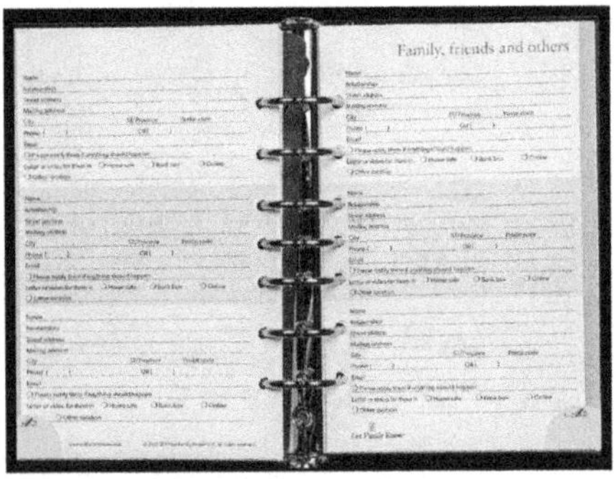

X-acto knife/box knife approach
Lay the book flat open and carefully cut the pages out

So the process goes smoothly, it may be helpful to watch a how-to video before you begin. Once pages are removed, use a paper punch to make holes that match the rings configuration of your binder.

Option
A local print shop or office products store can remove the pages and drill the holes for you, for a small fee.

Who do you want to pass your things on to?

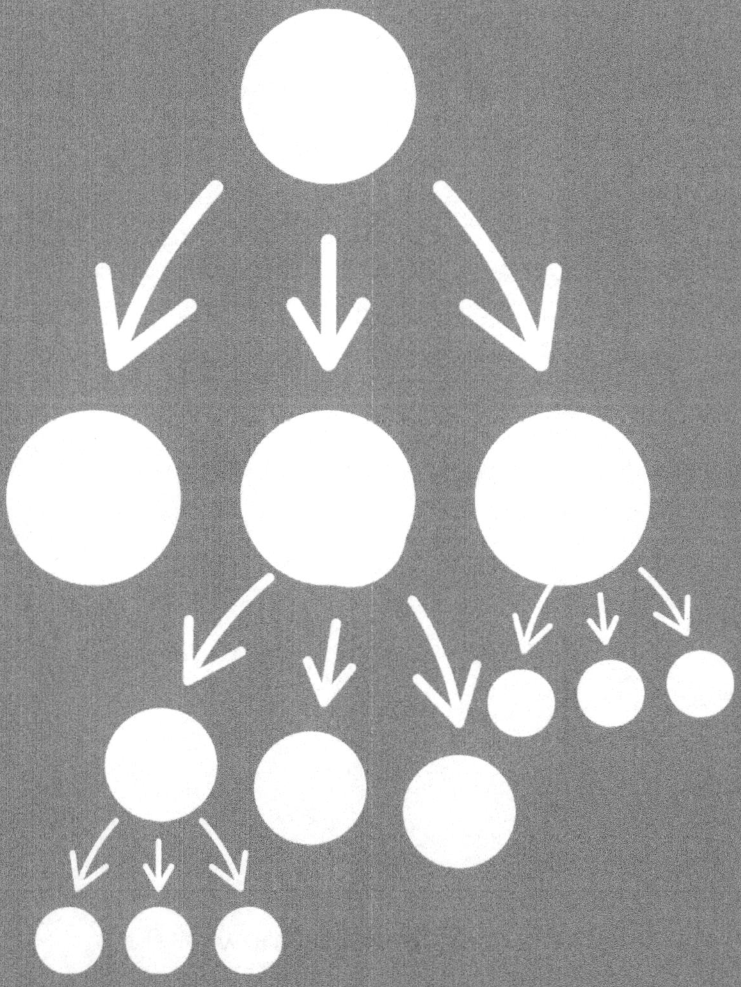

Let Family Know®

What I want you to have

I (we) want this person ______________________________

To have ______________________________

Here's why

Page ________ of ________

Let Family Know®

continued on next page

continued

I (we) want this person ____________________

____

To have ____________________

____

Page________ of________

Written by me ____________________ Date ____________

Witnessed by (optional) ____________________ Date ____________

❑ Check the box if this item is included in a will or other legal bequeathing document.

What I want you to have

I (we) want this person ______________________

____

To have ______________________

____

Here's why

Page______ of______

Let Family Know®

continued on next page

continued

I (we) want this person ______________________________

To have ______________________________

Page_______ of_______

Written by me______________________________ Date______________

Witnessed by (optional)______________________________ Date______________

❑ Check the box if this item is included in a will or other legal bequeathing document.

THIS IS NOT A WILL, is not legally binding, and should not be considered legal advice. This is intended for planning purposes and making wishes known.

What I want you to have

I (we) want this person ____________________

To have ____________________

Here's why

Page ______ of ______

Let Family Know®

continued on next page

continued

I (we) want this person ______________________________

____

To have ______________________________

____

Page________ of________

Written by me______________________________ Date________________

Witnessed by (optional)______________________________ Date________________

❑ Check the box if this item is included in a will or other legal bequeathing document.

What I want you to have

I (we) want this person ________________________________

____

To have ________________________________

____

Here's why

Let Family Know®

continued on next page

continued

I (we) want this person ______________________________

____

To have ______________________________

____

Page______ of______

Written by me______________________________ Date______________

Witnessed by (optional)______________________________ Date______________

☐ Check the box if this item is included in a will or other legal bequeathing document.

What I want you to have

I (we) want this person ______________________________

To have ______________________________

Here's why

Page______ of______

Let Family Know®

continued on next page

continued

I (we) want this person ______________________________

____

To have ______________________________

____

Page_______ of_______

Written by me______________________________ Date__________

Witnessed by (optional)______________________________ Date__________

❑ Check the box if this item is included in a will or other legal bequeathing document.

What I want you to have

I (we) want this person ______________________

To have ______________________

Here's why

Page ______ of ______

Let Family Know®

continued on next page

continued

I (we) want this person ______________________________

____

To have ______________________________

____

Page_______ of_______

Written by me______________________________ Date______________

Witnessed by (optional)______________________________ Date______________

❑ Check the box if this item is included in a will or other legal bequeathing document.

THIS IS NOT A WILL, is not legally binding, and should not be considered legal advice. This is intended for planning purposes and making wishes known.

What I want you to have

I (we) want this person

To have

Here's why

Page ______ of ______

Let Family Know®

continued on next page

continued

I (we) want this person ______________________________

____

To have ______________________________

____

Page________ of________

Written by me ______________________________ Date ____________

Witnessed by (optional) ______________________________ Date ____________

☐ Check the box if this item is included in a will or other legal bequeathing document.

THIS IS NOT A WILL, is not legally binding, and should not be considered legal advice. This is intended for planning purposes and making wishes known.

What I want you to have

I (we) want this person ______________________________

____

To have ______________________________

____

Here's why   Page ________ of ________

continued on next page

continued

I (we) want this person ______________________________

____

To have ______________________________

____

Page________ of________

Written by me______________________________ Date______________

Witnessed by (optional)______________________________ Date______________

❑ Check the box if this item is included in a will or other legal bequeathing document.

THIS IS NOT A WILL, is not legally binding, and should not be considered legal advice. This is intended for planning purposes and making wishes known.

What I want you to have

I (we) want this person ______________________

____

To have ______________________

____

Here's why

Page ________ of ________

continued on next page

continued

I (we) want this person ________________________________

____

To have ________________________________

____

Page________ of________

Written by me________________________________ Date________________

Witnessed by (optional)________________________________ Date________________

❑ Check the box if this item is included in a will or other legal bequeathing document.

THIS IS NOT A WILL, is not legally binding, and should not be considered legal advice. This is intended for planning purposes and making wishes known.

What I want you to have

I (we) want this person ______________________

To have ______________________

Here's why

Page ________ of ________

Let Family Know®

continued on next page

continued

I (we) want this person ______________________________

____

To have ______________________________

____

Page________ of________

Written by me ______________________________ Date ______________

Witnessed by (optional) ______________________________ Date ______________

❑ Check the box if this item is included in a will or other legal bequeathing document.

THIS IS NOT A WILL, is not legally binding, and should not be considered legal advice. This is intended for planning purposes and making wishes known.

What I want you to have

I (we) want this person ______________________

____

To have ______________________

____

Here's why

Page______ of______

continued on next page

continued

I (we) want this person ______

To have ______

Page______ of______

Written by me______ Date______

Witnessed by (optional)______ Date______

❑ Check the box if this item is included in a will or other legal bequeathing document.

THIS IS NOT A WILL, is not legally binding, and should not be considered legal advice. This is intended for planning purposes and making wishes known.

What I want you to have

I (we) want this person ______________________

____

To have ______________________

____

Here's why

Page________ of__________

continued on next page

continued

I (we) want this person ______________________

____

To have ______________________

____

Page______ of______

Written by me______________________ Date______________

Witnessed by (optional)______________________ Date______________

❑ Check the box if this item is included in a will or other legal bequeathing document.

THIS IS NOT A WILL, is not legally binding, and should not be considered legal advice. This is intended for planning purposes and making wishes known.

What I want you to have

I (we) want this person ______________________

To have ______________________

Here's why

continued on next page

continued

I (we) want this person ______________________________

____

To have ______________________________

____

Page________ of________

Written by me ______________________________ Date______________

Witnessed by (optional)______________________________ Date______________

❑ Check the box if this item is included in a will or other legal bequeathing document.

THIS IS NOT A WILL, is not legally binding, and should not be considered legal advice. This is intended for planning purposes and making wishes known.

What I want you to have

I (we) want this person ______________________________

____

To have ______________________________

____

Here's why

Page ________ of ________

continued on next page

continued

I (we) want this person ______________________________

____

To have ______________________________

____

Page ________ of ________

Written by me ______________________________ Date ______________

Witnessed by (optional) ______________________________ Date ______________

❑ Check the box if this item is included in a will or other legal bequeathing document.

THIS IS NOT A WILL, is not legally binding, and should not be considered legal advice. This is intended for planning purposes and making wishes known.

What I want you to have

I (we) want this person ______________________

To have ______________________

Here's why

Page ______ of ______

Let Family Know®

continued on next page

continued

I (we) want this person ____

To have ____

Page________ of________

Written by me______________________________ Date________________

Witnessed by (optional)______________________________ Date________________

❑ Check the box if this item is included in a will or other legal bequeathing document.

THIS IS NOT A WILL, is not legally binding, and should not be considered legal advice. This is intended for planning purposes and making wishes known.

What I want you to have

I (we) want this person ______________________

____

To have ______________________

____

Here's why

Page______ of______

continued on next page

continued

I (we) want this person ______________________________

To have ______________________________

Page______ of______

Written by me ______________________ Date ____________

Witnessed by (optional) ______________________ Date ____________

❑ Check the box if this item is included in a will or other legal bequeathing document.

THIS IS NOT A WILL, is not legally binding, and should not be considered legal advice. This is intended for planning purposes and making wishes known.

What I want you to have

I (we) want this person ______________________________

____

To have ______________________________

____

Here's why Page______ of______

continued on next page

continued

I (we) want this person ______________________________

____

To have ______________________________

____

Page______ of______

Written by me______________________________ Date______________

Witnessed by (optional)______________________________ Date______________

❑ Check the box if this item is included in a will or other legal bequeathing document.

THIS IS NOT A WILL, is not legally binding, and should not be considered legal advice. This is intended for planning purposes and making wishes known.

What I want you to have

I (we) want this person

To have

Here's why

Page ______ of ______

Let Family Know®

continued on next page

continued

I (we) want this person

To have

Page______ of______

Written by me______ Date______

Witnessed by (optional)______ Date______

❑ Check the box if this item is included in a will or other legal bequeathing document.

What I want you to have

I (we) want this person ______________________

To have ______________________

Here's why

Page ________ of ________

continued on next page

continued

I (we) want this person ______________________

To have ______________________

Page______ of______

Written by me ______________________ Date ______________________

Witnessed by (optional) ______________________ Date ______________________

☐ Check the box if this item is included in a will or other legal bequeathing document.

What I want you to have

I (we) want this person ______________________________

To have ______________________________

Here's why

Page ________ of ________

continued on next page

continued

I (we) want this person ______________________________

____

To have ______________________________

____

Page________ of________

Written by me______________________________ Date______________

Witnessed by (optional)______________________________ Date______________

❑ Check the box if this item is included in a will or other legal bequeathing document.

What I want you to have

I (we) want this person ______________________________

____

To have ______________________________

____

Here's why

Page ________ of ____________

continued on next page

continued

I (we) want this person ______________________________

To have ______________________________

Page______ of______

Written by me ______________________ Date ____________

Witnessed by (optional) ______________________ Date ____________

❑ Check the box if this item is included in a will or other legal bequeathing document.

THIS IS NOT A WILL, is not legally binding, and should not be considered legal advice. This is intended for planning purposes and making wishes known.

What I want you to have

I (we) want this person ______________________________

____

To have ______________________________

____

Here's why   Page______ of______

Let Family Know®

continued on next page

continued

I (we) want this person ____________________

____

To have ____________________

____

Page_______ of_______

Written by me ____________________ Date ____________________

Witnessed by (optional) ____________________ Date ____________________

❑ Check the box if this item is included in a will or other legal bequeathing document.

THIS IS NOT A WILL, is not legally binding, and should not be considered legal advice. This is intended for planning purposes and making wishes known.

What I want you to have

I (we) want this person ____________________

____

To have ____________________

____

Here's why

Page_______ of_______

Let Family Know®

continued on next page

continued

I (we) want this person ______________________________

____

To have ______________________________

____

Page_______ of_______

Written by me ______________________________ Date ______________

Witnessed by (optional) ______________________________ Date ______________

❑ Check the box if this item is included in a will or other legal bequeathing document.

THIS IS NOT A WILL, is not legally binding, and should not be considered legal advice. This is intended for planning purposes and making wishes known.

What I want you to have

I (we) want this person ______________________

____

To have ______________________

____

Here's why Page______ of______

continued on next page

continued

I (we) want this person

To have

Page ________ of ________

Written by me ____________________ Date ____________

Witnessed by (optional) ____________________ Date ____________

❑ Check the box if this item is included in a will or other legal bequeathing document.

THIS IS NOT A WILL, is not legally binding, and should not be considered legal advice. This is intended for planning purposes and making wishes known.

What I want you to have

I (we) want this person ____________________

To have ____________________

Here's why

continued on next page

continued

I (we) want this person ______________________________

____

To have ______________________________

____

Page ________ of ________

Written by me ______________________________ Date ______________

Witnessed by (optional) ______________________________ Date ______________

❑ Check the box if this item is included in a will or other legal bequeathing document.

What I want you to have

I (we) want this person ______________________

____

To have ______________________

____

Here's why

Page ________ of ________

Let Family Know®

continued on next page

continued

I (we) want this person ______________________________

____

To have ______________________________

____

Page________ of________

Written by me______________________________ Date______________

Witnessed by (optional)______________________________ Date______________

❑ Check the box if this item is included in a will or other legal bequeathing document.

THIS IS NOT A WILL, is not legally binding, and should not be considered legal advice. This is intended for planning purposes and making wishes known.

What I want you to have

I (we) want this person ______________________________

____

To have ______________________________

____

Here's why   Page_______ of_________

continued on next page

continued

I (we) want this person ____

To have ____

Page________ of________

Written by me______________________________ Date______________

Witnessed by (optional)__________________________ Date______________

❏ Check the box if this item is included in a will or other legal bequeathing document.

THIS IS NOT A WILL, is not legally binding, and should not be considered legal advice. This is intended for planning purposes and making wishes known.

What I want you to have

I (we) want this person ______________________________

____

To have ______________________________

____

Here's why

Page________ of____________

continued on next page

continued

I (we) want this person ________________________________

____

To have ________________________________

____

Page________ of________

Written by me ________________________________ Date ________________

Witnessed by (optional) ________________________________ Date ________________

☐ Check the box if this item is included in a will or other legal bequeathing document.

What I want you to have

I (we) want this person ______

To have ______

Here's why

Page ______ of ______

Let Family Know®

continued on next page

continued

I (we) want this person ________________________________

____

To have ________________________________

____

Page________ of________

Written by me________________________________ Date________________

Witnessed by (optional)________________________________ Date________________

❑ Check the box if this item is included in a will or other legal bequeathing document.

THIS IS NOT A WILL, is not legally binding, and should not be considered legal advice. This is intended for planning purposes and making wishes known.

What I want you to have

I (we) want this person ________________________________

____

To have ________________________________

____

Here's why

continued on next page

continued

I (we) want this person

To have

Page _______ of _______

Written by me ______________________________ Date ______________

Witnessed by (optional) __________________________ Date ______________

❑ Check the box if this item is included in a will or other legal bequeathing document.

THIS IS NOT A WILL, is not legally binding, and should not be considered legal advice. This is intended for planning purposes and making wishes known.

What I want you to have

I (we) want this person ______________________

To have ______________________

Here's why Page ______ of ______

Let Family Know®

continued on next page

continued

I (we) want this person ______________________________

____

To have ______________________________

____

Page________ of________

Written by me ______________________________ Date ______________

Witnessed by (optional) ______________________________ Date ______________

☐ Check the box if this item is included in a will or other legal bequeathing document.

THIS IS NOT A WILL, is not legally binding, and should not be considered legal advice. This is intended for planning purposes and making wishes known.

What I want you to have

I (we) want this person ______________________________

____

To have ______________________________

____

Here's why

continued on next page

continued

I (we) want this person ______________________________

____

To have ______________________________

____

Page________ of________

Written by me ______________________________ Date ______________

Witnessed by (optional) ______________________________ Date ______________

❑ Check the box if this item is included in a will or other legal bequeathing document.

THIS IS NOT A WILL, is not legally binding, and should not be considered legal advice. This is intended for planning purposes and making wishes known.

What I want you to have

I (we) want this person ______________________

____

To have ______________________

____

Here's why

Page________ of__________

Let Family Know®

continued on next page

continued

I (we) want this person ______________________

To have ______________________

Page_______ of_______

Written by me______________________ Date__________

Witnessed by (optional)______________________ Date__________

❑ Check the box if this item is included in a will or other legal bequeathing document.

THIS IS NOT A WILL, is not legally binding, and should not be considered legal advice. This is intended for planning purposes and making wishes known.

What I want you to have

I (we) want this person ______________________

To have ______________________

Here's why

Page ________ of ________

Let Family Know®

continued on next page

continued

I (we) want this person ______________________________

____

To have ______________________________

____

Page________ of________

Written by me ______________________________ Date ______________

Witnessed by (optional) ______________________________ Date ______________

❑ Check the box if this item is included in a will or other legal bequeathing document.

THIS IS NOT A WILL, is not legally binding, and should not be considered legal advice. This is intended for planning purposes and making wishes known.

What I want you to have

I (we) want this person ____________________

____

To have ____________________

____

Here's why

Page ________ of ________

continued on next page

continued

I (we) want this person ______________________________

____

To have ______________________________

____

Page________ of________

Written by me______________________________ Date______________

Witnessed by (optional)______________________________ Date______________

❑ Check the box if this item is included in a will or other legal bequeathing document.

THIS IS NOT A WILL, is not legally binding, and should not be considered legal advice. This is intended for planning purposes and making wishes known.

What I want you to have

I (we) want this person ______________________________

____

To have ______________________________

____

Here's why   Page_______ of_________

continued on next page

continued

I (we) want this person ______________________

____

To have ______________________

____

Page______ of______

Written by me______________________ Date______________

Witnessed by (optional)______________________ Date______________

❑ Check the box if this item is included in a will or other legal bequeathing document.

THIS IS NOT A WILL, is not legally binding, and should not be considered legal advice. This is intended for planning purposes and making wishes known.

What I want you to have

I (we) want this person ______________________________

____

To have ______________________________

____

Here's why   Page______ of ______

continued on next page

continued

I (we) want this person ______________________

To have ______________________

Page______ of______

Written by me______________________ Date______________

Witnessed by (optional)______________________ Date______________

☐ Check the box if this item is included in a will or other legal bequeathing document.

THIS IS NOT A WILL, is not legally binding, and should not be considered legal advice. This is intended for planning purposes and making wishes known.

What I want you to have

I (we) want this person ______________________

To have ______________________

Here's why

Page______ of______

Let Family Know®

continued on next page

continued

I (we) want this person ______________________________

To have ______________________________

Page________ of________

Written by me______________________________ Date______________

Witnessed by (optional)______________________________ Date______________

☐ Check the box if this item is included in a will or other legal bequeathing document.

THIS IS NOT A WILL, is not legally binding, and should not be considered legal advice. This is intended for planning purposes and making wishes known.

What I want you to have

I (we) want this person ______________________

____

To have ______________________

____

Here's why

continued on next page

continued

I (we) want this person ______________________

To have ______________________

Page________ of________

Written by me ______________________ Date ____________

Witnessed by (optional) ______________________ Date ____________

❑ Check the box if this item is included in a will or other legal bequeathing document.

THIS IS NOT A WILL, is not legally binding, and should not be considered legal advice. This is intended for planning purposes and making wishes known.

What I want you to have

I (we) want this person ______________________________

____

To have ______________________________

____

Here's why Page ________ of ____________

continued on next page

continued

I (we) want this person ____________________

____

To have ____________________

____

Page______ of______

Written by me ____________________ Date ____________

Witnessed by (optional) ____________________ Date ____________

❑ Check the box if this item is included in a will or other legal bequeathing document.

THIS IS NOT A WILL, is not legally binding, and should not be considered legal advice. This is intended for planning purposes and making wishes known.

What I want you to have

I (we) want this person ______________________________

To have ______________________________

Here's why

Page ________ of ________

continued on next page

continued

I (we) want this person ______________________

To have ______________________

Page________ of________

Written by me______________________ Date______________

Witnessed by (optional)______________________ Date______________

❑ Check the box if this item is included in a will or other legal bequeathing document.

What I want you to have

I (we) want this person ______________________

____

To have ______________________

____

Here's why

Page______ of______

continued on next page

continued

I (we) want this person ______________________

To have ______________________

Page_______ of_______

Written by me ______________________ Date ____________

Witnessed by (optional) ______________________ Date ____________

❑ Check the box if this item is included in a will or other legal bequeathing document.

What I want you to have

I (we) want this person ____________________

To have ____________________

Here's why

continued on next page

continued

I (we) want this person ____________________

____

To have ____________________

____

Page_______ of_______

Written by me ____________________ Date ____________

Witnessed by (optional) ____________________ Date ____________

❑ Check the box if this item is included in a will or other legal bequeathing document.

What I want you to have

I (we) want this person ____________________

To have ____________________

Here's why

Page ______ of ______

Let Family Know®

continued on next page

continued

I (we) want this person ______________________________

____

To have ______________________________

____

Page________ of________

Written by me______________________________ Date______________

Witnessed by (optional)______________________________ Date______________

❑ Check the box if this item is included in a will or other legal bequeathing document.

THIS IS NOT A WILL, is not legally binding, and should not be considered legal advice. This is intended for planning purposes and making wishes known.

What I want you to have

I (we) want this person ______________________

To have ______________________

Here's why

Page______ of______

Let Family Know®

continued on next page

continued

I (we) want this person ______________________________

____

To have ______________________________

____

Page______ of______

Written by me______________________________ Date______________

Witnessed by (optional)______________________________ Date______________

❑ Check the box if this item is included in a will or other legal bequeathing document.

THIS IS NOT A WILL, is not legally binding, and should not be considered legal advice. This is intended for planning purposes and making wishes known.

What I want you to have

I (we) want this person ______________________________

____

To have ______________________________

____

Here's why

Page________ of____________

____

____

____

____

____

____

____

____

____

____

____

____

____

____

____

____

____

____

____

____

____

____

continued on next page

continued

I (we) want this person ______________________________

____

To have ______________________________

____

Page______ of______

Written by me ______________________________ Date ______________

Witnessed by (optional) ______________________________ Date ______________

❑ Check the box if this item is included in a will or other legal bequeathing document.

What I want you to have

I (we) want this person

To have

Here's why

Page ______ of ______

Let Family Know®

continued on next page

continued

I (we) want this person ____________________

____

To have ____________________

____

Page ______ of ______

Written by me ____________________ Date __________

Witnessed by (optional) ____________________ Date __________

❑ Check the box if this item is included in a will or other legal bequeathing document.

THIS IS NOT A WILL, is not legally binding, and should not be considered legal advice. This is intended for planning purposes and making wishes known.

What I want you to have

I (we) want this person ______________________________

____

To have ______________________________

____

Here's why

Page________ of__________

Let Family Know®

continued on next page

continued

I (we) want this person ______________________________

____

To have ______________________________

____

Page________ of________

Written by me______________________________ Date______________

Witnessed by (optional)______________________________ Date______________

❑ Check the box if this item is included in a will or other legal bequeathing document.

THIS IS NOT A WILL, is not legally binding, and should not be considered legal advice. This is intended for planning purposes and making wishes known.

What I want you to have

I (we) want this person ______________________________

____

To have ______________________________

____

Here's why Page________ of____________

Let Family Know®

continued on next page

continued

I (we) want this person ____

To have ____

Page________ of________

Written by me______________________________ Date________________

Witnessed by (optional)__________________________ Date________________

❑ Check the box if this item is included in a will or other legal bequeathing document.

THIS IS NOT A WILL, is not legally binding, and should not be considered legal advice. This is intended for planning purposes and making wishes known.

What I want you to have

I (we) want this person ______________________

To have ______________________

Here's why

continued on next page

continued

I (we) want this person ______________________________

To have ______________________________

Page_______ of_______

Written by me______________________________ Date______________

Witnessed by (optional)______________________________ Date______________

❑ Check the box if this item is included in a will or other legal bequeathing document.

What I want you to have

I (we) want this person ____________________

____

To have ____________________

____

Here's why

Page________ of________

continued on next page

continued

I (we) want this person ______________________________

____

To have ______________________________

____

Page_______ of_______

Written by me ______________________________ Date______________

Witnessed by (optional)______________________________ Date______________

❑ Check the box if this item is included in a will or other legal bequeathing document.

THIS IS NOT A WILL, is not legally binding, and should not be considered legal advice. This is intended for planning purposes and making wishes known.

What I want you to have

I (we) want this person ______________________________

____

To have ______________________________

____

Here's why Page ________ of ________

Let Family Know®

continued on next page

continued

I (we) want this person ______________________________

____

To have ______________________________

____

Page________ of________

Written by me ______________________________ Date ______________

Witnessed by (optional) ______________________________ Date ______________

❑ Check the box if this item is included in a will or other legal bequeathing document.

What I want you to have

I (we) want this person ______________________________

To have ______________________________

Here's why

Page________ of__________

Let Family Know®

continued on next page

continued

I (we) want this person ______________________________

To have ______________________________

Page______ of______

Written by me______________________________ Date______________

Witnessed by (optional)______________________________ Date______________

❑ Check the box if this item is included in a will or other legal bequeathing document.

What I want you to have

I (we) want this person ______________________________

____

To have ______________________________

____

Here's why

continued on next page

continued

I (we) want this person ______________________________

____

To have ______________________________

____

Page______ of______

Written by me ______________________________ Date ______________

Witnessed by (optional) ______________________________ Date ______________

❑ Check the box if this item is included in a will or other legal bequeathing document.

THIS IS NOT A WILL, is not legally binding, and should not be considered legal advice. This is intended for planning purposes and making wishes known.

What I want you to have

I (we) want this person ________________________________

____

To have ________________________________

____

Here's why Page ________ of ________

Let Family Know®

continued on next page

continued

I (we) want this person ______________________________

____

To have ______________________________

____

Page_______ of_______

Written by me ______________________________ Date ______________

Witnessed by (optional) ______________________________ Date ______________

❑ Check the box if this item is included in a will or other legal bequeathing document.

THIS IS NOT A WILL, is not legally binding, and should not be considered legal advice. This is intended for planning purposes and making wishes known.

What I want you to have

I (we) want this person ______________________________

____

To have ______________________________

____

Here's why Page______ of______

continued on next page

continued

I (we) want this person ____________________________

To have ____________________________

Page________ of________

Written by me____________________________ Date________________

Witnessed by (optional)____________________________ Date________________

❑ Check the box if this item is included in a will or other legal bequeathing document.

What I want you to have

I (we) want this person ______________________

To have ______________________

Here's why

Page ________ of ________

Let Family Know®

continued on next page

continued

I (we) want this person ______________________

To have ______________________

Page______ of______

Written by me ______________________ Date ______________

Witnessed by (optional) ______________________ Date ______________

❑ Check the box if this item is included in a will or other legal bequeathing document.

THIS IS NOT A WILL, is not legally binding, and should not be considered legal advice. This is intended for planning purposes and making wishes known.

What I want you to have

I (we) want this person ______________________________

____

To have ______________________________

____

Here's why Page________ of__________

continued on next page

continued

I (we) want this person ______________________

____

To have ______________________

____

Page______ of______

Written by me______________________ Date______________

Witnessed by (optional)______________________ Date______________

❑ Check the box if this item is included in a will or other legal bequeathing document.

THIS IS NOT A WILL, is not legally binding, and should not be considered legal advice. This is intended for planning purposes and making wishes known.

What I want you to have

I (we) want this person ______________________________

To have ______________________________

Here's why

Page ______ of ______

Let Family Know®

continued on next page

continued

I (we) want this person ______________________

To have ______________________

Page ______ of ______

Written by me ______________________ Date ______________________

Witnessed by (optional) ______________________ Date ______________________

❑ Check the box if this item is included in a will or other legal bequeathing document.

What I want you to have

I (we) want this person ____________________

To have ____________________

Here's why

Page ________ of ________

Let Family Know®

continued on next page

continued

I (we) want this person ______________________

To have ______________________

Page ______ of ______

Written by me ______________________ Date ______

Witnessed by (optional) ______________________ Date ______

❑ Check the box if this item is included in a will or other legal bequeathing document.

What I want you to have

I (we) want this person ______________________________

To have ______________________________

Here's why

Page______ of______

Let Family Know®

continued on next page

continued

I (we) want this person ____________________

____

To have ____________________

____

Page______ of______

Written by me____________________ Date____________

Witnessed by (optional)____________________ Date____________

☐ Check the box if this item is included in a will or other legal bequeathing document.

What I want you to have

I (we) want this person

To have

Here's why

Page ________ of ________

Let Family Know®

continued on next page

continued

I (we) want this person ____

____

To have ____

____

Page________ of________

Written by me____ Date________________

Witnessed by (optional)________________________________ Date________________

❑ Check the box if this item is included in a will or other legal bequeathing document.

What I want you to have

I (we) want this person ____________________

To have ____________________

Here's why

Let Family Know®

continued on next page

continued

I (we) want this person ______________________________

____

To have ______________________________

____

Page_______ of_______

Written by me ______________________________ Date ____________

Witnessed by (optional) ______________________________ Date ____________

❑ Check the box if this item is included in a will or other legal bequeathing document.

What I want you to have

I (we) want this person ____________________

To have ____________________

Here's why

Page ________ of ________

continued on next page

continued

I (we) want this person ______________________

____

To have ______________________

____

Page______ of______

Written by me ______________________ Date ______________

Witnessed by (optional) ______________________ Date ______________

❑ Check the box if this item is included in a will or other legal bequeathing document.

What I want you to have

I (we) want this person

To have

Here's why

Page ______ of ______

Let Family Know®

continued on next page

continued

I (we) want this person ______________________________

____

To have ______________________________

____

Page________ of________

Written by me ______________________________ Date ______________

Witnessed by (optional) ______________________________ Date ______________

❑ Check the box if this item is included in a will or other legal bequeathing document.

THIS IS NOT A WILL, is not legally binding, and should not be considered legal advice. This is intended for planning purposes and making wishes known.

What I want you to have

I (we) want this person ______________________

To have ______________________

Here's why

continued on next page

continued

I (we) want this person ______________________________

____

To have ______________________________

____

Page________ of________

Written by me ______________________________ Date ______________

Witnessed by (optional) ______________________________ Date ______________

❑ Check the box if this item is included in a will or other legal bequeathing document.

What I want you to have

I (we) want this person ______________________

To have ______________________

Here's why

Page ________ of ________

Let Family Know®

continued on next page

continued

I (we) want this person ______________________________

____

To have ______________________________

____

Page________ of________

Written by me______________________________ Date______________

Witnessed by (optional)______________________________ Date______________

❑ Check the box if this item is included in a will or other legal bequeathing document.

THIS IS NOT A WILL, is not legally binding, and should not be considered legal advice. This is intended for planning purposes and making wishes known.

What I want you to have

I (we) want this person ______________________________

____

To have ______________________________

____

Here's why Page________ of__________

continued on next page

continued

I (we) want this person ______________________________

To have ______________________________

Page________ of________

Written by me ______________________________ Date ______________

Witnessed by (optional) ______________________________ Date ______________

❑ Check the box if this item is included in a will or other legal bequeathing document.

THIS IS NOT A WILL, is not legally binding, and should not be considered legal advice. This is intended for planning purposes and making wishes known.

What I want you to have

I (we) want this person ______________________________

To have ______________________________

Here's why

Let Family Know®

continued on next page

continued

I (we) want this person ____________________

To have ____________________

Page_______ of_______

Written by me ____________________ Date ____________

Witnessed by (optional) ____________________ Date ____________

❑ Check the box if this item is included in a will or other legal bequeathing document.

What I want you to have

I (we) want this person ______________________

To have ______________________

Here's why

Page______ of______

continued on next page

continued

I (we) want this person ______________________________

____

To have ______________________________

____

Page________ of________

Written by me ______________________________ Date ______________

Witnessed by (optional) ______________________________ Date ______________

❑ Check the box if this item is included in a will or other legal bequeathing document.

THIS IS NOT A WILL, is not legally binding, and should not be considered legal advice. This is intended for planning purposes and making wishes known.

What I want you to have

I (we) want this person ______________________________

____

To have ______________________________

____

Here's why

continued on next page

continued

I (we) want this person ____________________

____

To have ____________________

____

Page________ of________

Written by me ____________________ Date ____________

Witnessed by (optional) ____________________ Date ____________

❑ Check the box if this item is included in a will or other legal bequeathing document.

THIS IS NOT A WILL, is not legally binding, and should not be considered legal advice. This is intended for planning purposes and making wishes known.

What I want you to have

I (we) want this person ______________________________

To have ______________________________

Here's why

continued on next page

continued

I (we) want this person ______________________________

____

To have ______________________________

____

Page________ of________

Written by me______________________________ Date________________

Witnessed by (optional)______________________________ Date________________

❑ Check the box if this item is included in a will or other legal bequeathing document.

What I want you to have

I (we) want this person ________________________________

____

To have ________________________________

____

Here's why

Let Family Know®

continued on next page

continued

I (we) want this person ______________________________

To have ______________________________

Page________ of________

Written by me ______________________________ Date ______________

Witnessed by (optional) ______________________________ Date ______________

❑ Check the box if this item is included in a will or other legal bequeathing document.

What I want you to have

I (we) want this person ______________________________

____

To have ______________________________

____

Here's why

Page________ of____________

continued on next page

continued

I (we) want this person ______________________________

____

To have ______________________________

____

Page ________ of ________

Written by me ______________________________ Date ______________

Witnessed by (optional) ______________________________ Date ______________

❑ Check the box if this item is included in a will or other legal bequeathing document.

What I want you to have

I (we) want this person ______________________________

____

To have ______________________________

____

Here's why

continued on next page

continued

I (we) want this person ____________________

To have ____________________

Page ____ of ____

Written by me ____________________ Date ____________

Witnessed by (optional) ____________________ Date ____________

❑ Check the box if this item is included in a will or other legal bequeathing document.

What I want you to have

I (we) want this person ______________________________

To have ______________________________

Here's why

Page ________ of ________

Let Family Know®

continued on next page

continued

I (we) want this person ____________________

____

To have ____________________

____

Page______ of______

Written by me ____________________ Date ____________

Witnessed by (optional) ____________________ Date ____________

☐ Check the box if this item is included in a will or other legal bequeathing document.

THIS IS NOT A WILL, is not legally binding, and should not be considered legal advice. This is intended for planning purposes and making wishes known.

What I want you to have

I (we) want this person ______________________

To have ______________________

Here's why

continued on next page

continued

I (we) want this person ________________________________

____

To have ________________________________

____

Page________ of________

Written by me________________________________ Date________________

Witnessed by (optional)________________________________ Date________________

❑ Check the box if this item is included in a will or other legal bequeathing document.

THIS IS NOT A WILL, is not legally binding, and should not be considered legal advice. This is intended for planning purposes and making wishes known.

What I want you to have

I (we) want this person ________________________________

____

To have ________________________________

____

Here's why

Page________ of________

Let Family Know®

continued on next page

continued

I (we) want this person ______________________________

To have ______________________________

Page______ of______

Written by me ______________________________ Date ______________

Witnessed by (optional) ______________________________ Date ______________

❑ Check the box if this item is included in a will or other legal bequeathing document.

What I want you to have

I (we) want this person ______________________

To have ______________________

Here's why

continued on next page

continued

I (we) want this person ______________________

To have ______________________

Page______ of______

Written by me ______________________ Date ______________

Witnessed by (optional) ______________________ Date ______________

☐ Check the box if this item is included in a will or other legal bequeathing document.

THIS IS NOT A WILL, is not legally binding, and should not be considered legal advice. This is intended for planning purposes and making wishes known.

What I want you to have

I (we) want this person ______________________

To have ______________________

Here's why

Page______ of ______

continued on next page

continued

I (we) want this person ______________________

____

To have ______________________

____

Page______ of______

Written by me ______________________ Date______

Witnessed by (optional) ______________________ Date______

❑ Check the box if this item is included in a will or other legal bequeathing document.

THIS IS NOT A WILL, is not legally binding, and should not be considered legal advice. This is intended for planning purposes and making wishes known.

What I want you to have

I (we) want this person ______________________

____

To have ______________________

____

Here's why

Page ________ of ________

Let Family Know®

continued on next page

continued

I (we) want this person ______________________________

____

To have ______________________________

____

Page________ of________

Written by me ______________________________ Date ______________

Witnessed by (optional) ______________________________ Date ______________

❑ Check the box if this item is included in a will or other legal bequeathing document.

THIS IS NOT A WILL, is not legally binding, and should not be considered legal advice. This is intended for planning purposes and making wishes known.

What I want you to have

I (we) want this person ______________________

____

To have ______________________

____

Here's why Page_______ of__________

Let Family Know®

continued on next page

continued

I (we) want this person ______________________________

____

To have ______________________________

____

Page________ of________

Written by me ______________________________ Date ______________

Witnessed by (optional) ______________________________ Date ______________

❑ Check the box if this item is included in a will or other legal bequeathing document.

What I want you to have

I (we) want this person ______________________

To have ______________________

Here's why

Page ________ of ________

Let Family Know®

continued on next page

continued

I (we) want this person ______________________________

____

To have ______________________________

____

Page________ of________

Written by me ______________________________ Date ______________

Witnessed by (optional) ______________________________ Date ______________

❑ Check the box if this item is included in a will or other legal bequeathing document.

What I want you to have

I (we) want this person ______________________________

____

To have ______________________________

____

Here's why

Page______ of________

continued on next page

continued

I (we) want this person ______________________________

To have ______________________________

Page ________ of ________

Written by me ______________________________ Date ____________

Witnessed by (optional) ______________________________ Date ____________

❑ Check the box if this item is included in a will or other legal bequeathing document.

What I want you to have

I (we) want this person

To have

Here's why

Page ______ of ______

Let Family Know®

continued on next page

continued

I (we) want this person ______________________________

____

To have ______________________________

____

Page________ of________

Written by me ______________________________ Date ______________

Witnessed by (optional) ______________________________ Date ______________

❑ Check the box if this item is included in a will or other legal bequeathing document.

THIS IS NOT A WILL, is not legally binding, and should not be considered legal advice. This is intended for planning purposes and making wishes known.

What I want you to have

I (we) want this person ______________________________

To have ______________________________

Here's why

Page________ of__________

Let Family Know®

continued on next page

continued

I (we) want this person ______________________________

To have ______________________________

Page________ of________

Written by me ______________________ Date __________

Witnessed by (optional) ______________________ Date __________

❑ Check the box if this item is included in a will or other legal bequeathing document.

What I want you to have

I (we) want this person ______________________________

To have ______________________________

Here's why

Page ________ of ____________

Let Family Know®

continued on next page

continued

I (we) want this person ______________________________

____

To have ______________________________

____

Page________ of________

Written by me ______________________________ Date ______________

Witnessed by (optional) ______________________________ Date ______________

❑ Check the box if this item is included in a will or other legal bequeathing document.

THIS IS NOT A WILL, is not legally binding, and should not be considered legal advice. This is intended for planning purposes and making wishes known.

What I want you to have

I (we) want this person ______

______

To have ______

______

Here's why

Page ______ of ______

continued on next page

continued

I (we) want this person ______________________________________

To have ____

Page________ of________

Written by me____________________________ Date______________

Witnessed by (optional)________________________ Date______________

☐ Check the box if this item is included in a will or other legal bequeathing document.

What I want you to have

I (we) want this person ______________________

____

To have ______________________

____

Here's why

Page________ of__________

continued on next page

continued

I (we) want this person

To have

Page ______ of ______

Written by me ____________________ Date ____________

Witnessed by (optional) ____________________ Date ____________

❑ Check the box if this item is included in a will or other legal bequeathing document.

THIS IS NOT A WILL, is not legally binding, and should not be considered legal advice. This is intended for planning purposes and making wishes known.

What I want you to have

I (we) want this person ______________________

To have ______________________

Here's why

Page ______ of ______

Let Family Know®

continued on next page

continued

I (we) want this person ____________________

____

To have ____________________

____

Page ______ of ______

Written by me ____________________ Date ____________

Witnessed by (optional) ____________________ Date ____________

❑ Check the box if this item is included in a will or other legal bequeathing document.

THIS IS NOT A WILL, is not legally binding, and should not be considered legal advice. This is intended for planning purposes and making wishes known.

What I want you to have

I (we) want this person ______________________________

____

To have ______________________________

____

Here's why

Page________ of____________

Let Family Know®

continued on next page

continued

I (we) want this person ______________________

To have ______________________

Page_______ of_______

Written by me ______________________ Date ____________

Witnessed by (optional) ______________________ Date ____________

❑ Check the box if this item is included in a will or other legal bequeathing document.

THIS IS NOT A WILL, is not legally binding, and should not be considered legal advice. This is intended for planning purposes and making wishes known.

What I want you to have

I (we) want this person ______________________

To have ______________________

Here's why

Let Family Know®

continued on next page

continued

I (we) want this person ______________________________

____

To have ______________________________

____

Page_______ of_______

Written by me ______________________________ Date ______________

Witnessed by (optional) ______________________________ Date ______________

❏ Check the box if this item is included in a will or other legal bequeathing document.

What I want you to have

I (we) want this person ______________________

To have ______________________

Here's why

Page ______ of ______

Let Family Know®

continued on next page

continued

I (we) want this person ______________________________

To have ______________________________

Page______ of______

Written by me ______________________ Date ______________

Witnessed by (optional) ______________________ Date ______________

❑ Check the box if this item is included in a will or other legal bequeathing document.

What I want you to have

I (we) want this person

To have

Here's why

Page ______ of ______

Let Family Know®

continued on next page

continued

I (we) want this person ______________________________

____

To have ______________________________

____

Page________ of________

Written by me ______________________________ Date ______________

Witnessed by (optional) ______________________________ Date ______________

❑ Check the box if this item is included in a will or other legal bequeathing document.

THIS IS NOT A WILL, is not legally binding, and should not be considered legal advice. This is intended for planning purposes and making wishes known.

IMPORTANT ... PLEASE READ

TERMS OF USE

The Let Family Know® books, journals, planners, and organizers are sold with the understanding that the publisher is not engaged in providing legal, accounting or other professional service. Use of the products and websites produced by Let Family Know® LLC do not constitute legal advice—but rather, they are tools designed to simplify and make easier, the creation of information you would want people to know if anything should happen that would end your life or render you unable to communicate or make decisions. The journals, planners and organizers offer simple, fill-in-the-blank forms and pages that are not prepared nor customized by Let Family Know to meet any one person's particular needs.

We are not licensed to practice law, nor do we imply that these tools can substitute for legal advice. Where legal matters are concerned, we urge you to seek advice from a professional attorney who is licensed to practice law in the state in which you reside. Or, when looking for expert assistance on protecting your estate, your heirs or finances, consult with an estate attorney or professional estate planner who knows the laws in your state (as every state has different laws governing wills and estates), and who can help you design a plan to achieve the outcome you desire.

Let Family Know® tools, information and products are not intended to create or imply any attorney-client relationship.

NO WARRANTY. THIS PLANNER AND ITS FORMS ARE PROVIDED ON AN "AS IS" BASIS. TO THE FULLEST EXTENT PERMITTED BY LAW, Let Family Know® LLC expressly disclaims any warranty of any kind, whether express or implied,about the warranty of merchantability, fitness for a particular purpose, title and non-infringement.

Let Family Know® LLC makes no warranty that (A) the books, journals, planners, organizers or information will meet your requirements; (B) that the results that may be obtained from the use of the materials will be accurate or reliable; or (C) the quality of the products or information, or other material or services purchased from the company by you will meet your expectations.

Obtaining this Planner or any materials from Let Family Know LLC, is done at your own discretion and at your own risk. Let Family Know LLC, and its publishers, shall have no responsibility.

Continued ...

LIMITATION OF LIABILITY AND INDEMNIFICATION

You will hold Let Family Know LLC and its officers, directors, employees and agents harmless for any indirect, punitive, special, incidental, or consequential damage, however it arises (including attorney's fees and all related costs and expenses of litigation and arbitration or arbitration instituted), whether in an action of contract, negligence, or other tortuous action, or arising out of or in connection with this agreement, including without limitation any claim for personal injury or property damage, arising form this agreement, and any violation by me of any Federal, State or Local laws, statutes, rules or regulations, even if Let Family Know had been previously advised of the possibility of such damage. If there is liability found on the part of Let Family Know LLC, it will be limited to the amount paid for the products and/or services and under no circumstances will there be consequential or punative damages. Some states do not allow the exclusion or limitation of incidental or consequential damages, so the above limitation or exclusion may not apply to me. Further, except as permitted by law, nothing in this paragraph is intended to modify the provisions of California business and Professions Code Sections 6400, ET SEQ.

ACKNOWLEDGEMENT

*** By using Let Family Know® products or services, you acknowledge you have read these terms of use and agree to be bound by them.

More titles from Let Family Know®

8.5″ x 11″ books with planning worksheets or forms

How to Keep Family Stories, Traditions, and Values from Fading: *Recall and record years of your life ... in just minutes each week.*

How to Decide Who Will Inherit Your Stuff: *7 basic estate-planning steps that turn procrastination into peace of mind.*

Dear ________, *A guide to writing the very best legacy letter possible.*

Planning for Your Pets: *If something were to happen to you, what would happen to them?*

Handwritten Letters to Your Grandchildren: *a keepsake they will treasure their whole life long.*

More titles from Let Family Know®

5.5″ x 8.5″ planners, journals, organizers, keepers

My Important Information ORGANIZER

What I Want You to Have PLANNER

What I Want You to Know JOURNAL

Family, Friends and Others ORGANIZER

My Digital Life USERNAME/PASSWORD ORGANIZER

My Digital Life PRIVATE ACCESS KEEPER

Made in the USA
Monee, IL
04 November 2026

67377687R00115